MONUMENTAL MILESTONES
GREAT EVENTS OF MODERN TIMES

The Russian Revolution, 1917

Alexander Kerensky (left) reviews the troops in 1917.

Mitchell Lane
PUBLISHERS

P.O. Box 196
Hockessin, Delaware 19707

Titles in the Series

MONUMENTAL MILESTONES
GREAT EVENTS OF MODERN TIMES

The Russian Revolution, 1917

Vladimir Lenin addresses the crowd in Red Square following the Russian Revolution.

Jim Whiting

Printing   1   2   3   4   5   6   7   8   9

Library of Congress Cataloging-in-Publication Data
Whiting, Jim, 1943–
    The Russian Revolution : 1917 / by Jim Whiting.
        p. cm. — (Monumental milestones)
    Includes bibliographical references and index.
    ISBN-13: 978-1-58415-537-9 (library bound)
    1. Soviet Union—History—Revolution, 1917–1921—Juvenile literature. I. Title.
DK265.W43 2007
947.084'1—dc22
                                                                                2007000778

947.084
Whiting

ABOUT THE AUTHOR: Jim Whiting has been a remarkably versatile and accomplished journalist, writer, editor, and photographer for more than 30 years. A voracious reader since early childhood, Mr. Whiting has written and edited more than 250 nonfiction children's books on a wide range of topics, including *An Overview of World War I*, *The Scopes Monkey Trial*, and *The Creation of Israel*. He lives in Washington state with his wife and two teenage sons.

PHOTO CREDITS: Cover, pp. 1, 3, 12, 15, 21, 24—JupiterImages; p. 29—Sharon Beck; p. 34—Hulton Archives; p. 38—Library of Congress; p. 40—Corbis; p. 41—Evstafiev Mikhail.

NOTE ON DATES: Roman Emperor Julius Caesar adopted what is known as the Julian calendar in 45 BCE. Over the succeeding centuries, it proved to be inaccurate. In 1582, Pope Gregory XIII approved the more accurate Gregorian calendar. Besides adjusting the yearly calendar, it skipped thirteen days the year it was approved. By the middle of the eighteenth century, the Gregorian calendar had been adopted almost everywhere. Russia was a notable exception. One of the earliest acts of the new Soviet government was to adopt the Gregorian calendar on January 31, 1918. The following day was February 14.

    As a result, events leading up to and including the Russian Revolution are often expressed in two dates: Old Style (Julian calendar) and New Style (Gregorian calendar). This book takes the approach of many historians: Dates of events inside Russia are shown as Old Style before the change, then as New Style afterward. Dates of events outside Russia are indicated in New Style.

Contents

The Russian Revolution, 1917

Jim Whiting

*For Your Information

Czar Alexander II was assassinated on March 13, 1881, by a group of revolutionaries.

A man threw a bomb at the czar's carriage. His aim was off and he wounded several of the czar's guards. As Alexander got out to check the condition of the wounded men, another man (at left) hurled a bomb at the czar's feet. The explosion killed him.

CHAPTER 1

The Death of a Brother

It was still dark when the prison guard roughly shook Alexander Ulyanov awake. "You will be hanged in two hours," the man said.

The twenty-one-year-old's impending death was a shock to many people. He came from a prosperous and important family in Simbirsk, Russia. When he graduated from high school, he received a gold medal. He did just as well when he became a university student. He studied zoology and won another gold medal for his research work with worms.

The university Alexander attended was in St. Petersburg, the capital of Russia. For centuries, the country had been under the rule of all-powerful czars. Their regimes were often harsh and cruel. Early in the nineteenth century, secret societies began emerging. Their aim was to make changes in Russia. They wanted a less oppressive government, one more open to the will of the people. Their strategies increasingly turned to violence. A group called the People's Will was formed in 1879. Their goal was to assassinate Czar Alexander II. They succeeded two years later.

After the assassination, Russian secret police carefully watched people for any signs of trouble. Late in 1886, several of Alexander Ulyanov's friends were sent to do hard labor in Siberia. This created a dilemma for the young man. He could remain politically uninvolved and continue what seemed to be a secure and respected career in science, or he could join the movement toward revolution. *Das Kapital*, a book by Karl Marx, helped him make up his mind.

The czars used censorship to prevent radical ideas from getting into Russia. Books that the censors thought were dangerous could not be published there. In 1872, a Russian publisher gave the censors a copy of *Das Kapital*. The censors knew Marx's ideas were radical. All of his previous writings, including his *Communist Manifesto*, had been banned in Russia.

Five of the assassins of Alexander II were hanged on April 3, 1881.

The plotters made several attempts on the czar's life before they succeeded. In one, they planted a bomb at a state dinner. Sixty-seven people were killed or injured.

Communist Manifesto laid out a radical plan for changing government. At that time, most Western European countries operated under a capitalist system. A relatively few capitalists (owners) controlled factories and other means of production. They hired people to work for them. In this system, owners were wealthy and workers lived in poverty.

Some people wanted to change the capitalist system. They believed in socialism, a system in which the workers controlled the means of production. As a result, everyone would earn enough money to live comfortably. Extreme wealth and extreme poverty would disappear.

In his *Manifesto*, Marx went even further. He advocated communism, the belief that there would be no need for government after a period of socialism and reeducation. People would work for the common good rather than for their own selfish ends. They would have what they needed for a good life. There would be no more national governments and no more wars.

Because of Marx's extreme views, the Russian publisher of *Das Kapital* expected the censors to ban it. To his astonishment, two censors approved it for printing. "It is possible to state with certainty that very few people in Russia will read it, and even fewer will understand it,"[1] said one.

The other one said that Marx's book was based on an analysis of the capitalist economic system of Western Europe. Russia was still an agricultural society with little industry. No one would pay attention to it.

Both men were mistaken. *Das Kapital* became a sensation. Until then, Russian revolutionaries had placed their hopes on the rural peasants, but the peasants didn't seem to understand their cause. After reading *Das Kapital*, the revolutionaries could recruit the working-class people in the cities. These workers would be more likely to support them.

Reading Marx helped Alexander Ulyanov decide to commit to the revolutionary cause in St. Petersburg. He and his friends plotted to assassinate Czar

Alexander prepared grenades packed with nitroglycerin and scores of small metal balls. He and his fellow plotters planned to use them to assassinate Czar Alexander III. The group also hollowed out dictionaries and filled the space with dynamite.

Alexander Ulyanov

Alexander III on the sixth anniversary of the death of the czar's father. They thought this deed would lead to reforms and a better life for the Russian people.

They were no match for the czar's secret police. More than seventy revolutionaries, including Ulyanov, were arrested. When the group went to trial, most of the plotters pleaded for their lives. They were sentenced to hard labor. Alexander and four others refused to back down. Tearfully, Alexander's mother begged him to reconsider. Firmly, he told her, "I cannot do it after everything I said in court. It would be insincere. Imagine, Mama, two men facing each other at a duel. One of them has already shot at his opponent, the other has yet to do so, when the one who has shot asks him not to. No, I cannot behave like that!"[2]

In the predawn darkness of May 8, 1887, the five young men went bravely to their deaths.

As Alexander died, his seventeen-year-old brother, Vladimir, was taking exams at his school in Simbirsk, nearly 1,000 miles from St. Petersburg. Vladimir was a model student with little interest in politics. He never gave "cause for dissatisfaction, by word or by deed, to the school authorities," wrote the headmaster, Fedor Kerensky. "Religion and discipline were the basis of this upbringing."[3]

Vladimir would also become a revolutionary—and be far more successful in achieving his goal than his brother had been. He would become the leading figure in a revolution that established an entirely new form of government for Russia. The roots of this revolution had been growing for many years. In just over six months in 1917, Vladimir would take over its leadership. He would take the revolution in a direction that few people could have foreseen.

Many other governments were shocked at the changes he made. They bitterly opposed his ideas.

The new government would survive. Soon its beliefs would spread around the world. Other countries would adopt a similar type of government.

By that time, Vladimir Ulyanov had changed his name. Through his work with the Russian Revolution, he would become immortalized as Vladimir Lenin. For several decades, the city where his brother died would be called Leningrad in Vladimir's honor.

After Lenin's death, he would receive the same high honor accorded to ancient Egyptian pharaohs. His mummified body would lie beneath a sealed glass case so that visitors from all over the world could see it.

Alexander Kerensky was born in Simbirsk in 1881. When he was eight, his father, Fedor Kerensky, became chief inspector of schools in the city of Tashkent, and Alexander attended school there. As was the case with his future rival Lenin, there was "nothing at this stage to suggest the future career of Kerensky as a minister of the revolution," said one of his teachers. "He happily complied with the strict discipline of the school, went enthusiastically to church, and even sang in the church choir."[4]

As a teenager, he was especially interested in acting. He became involved in revolutionary activities when he entered St. Petersburg University. He graduated from law school and became an attorney in 1904. Many of his clients were people accused of illegal revolutionary activities.

Alexander Kerensky

He entered politics with his election to the Duma (a form of parliament) in 1912. Regarded as a moderate, a man especially interested in supporting better conditions for working people, he advanced quickly.

When the February Revolution broke out in 1917, he became even more important. As the Minister of Justice in the Provisional Government, he announced an ambitious plan of civil liberties that included the right to vote and freedom of the press. Four months later he was the prime minister.

His efforts to keep the war going led to his demise. After the Bolsheviks took over the Provisional Government, he hid for several weeks before escaping to Paris. He remained until the German takeover in 1940 during World War II. He then traveled to the United States, where he made radio broadcasts supporting the Soviet government against the Germans.

He spent nearly all of his remaining life in the United States, working as an author and a teacher. He died in New York in 1970.

Because of Kerensky's efforts in overthrowing the czar, the Russian Orthodox churches in New York refused to allow him to be buried in their cemeteries. Church leaders were unhappy because the government that was installed after the revolution opposed their religion. Finally his body was flown to London. He was laid to rest in a cemetery that didn't have any religious affiliations.

Emperor Nicholas I, born in 1796, succeeded his brother Alexander I as czar in December 1825.

Nicholas believed in absolute power and offered to help the rulers in other countries suppress revolutions when they broke out. As a result, he was nicknamed the "gendarme [policeman] of Europe."

CHAPTER 2

The Roots of Revolution

Although the Russian Revolution occurred in 1917, its recorded roots reach back more than a thousand years to the time that Russia was founded. Vikings under a leader named Rurik established settlements and took control over Slavic tribes in Eastern Europe in the middle of the ninth century. Eventually these people became known as Rus. By the eleventh century their capital of Kiev was the largest and most prosperous city in Europe.

Soon afterward, Mongols from Asia invaded Rus and began a rule that lasted for hundreds of years. They granted control of Muscovy (the lands surrounding the present-day city of Moscow) to a branch of Rurik's family.

When Mongol rule ended in the fifteenth century, these descendants of Rurik began expanding their territory. Ivan III (also known as Ivan the Great) gave himself the title of czar. Also spelled *tsar,* the term comes from the Latin word *caesar,* which means "ruler." To the czars, *ruling* implied absolute control. Ivan set out to regain all of the lands of Rus (Russia) that had been under Mongol control. By his death in 1505, he had tripled his original lands.

His grandson, Ivan IV, became czar at age three in 1533. Eventually acquiring the nickname of Ivan the Terrible, he expanded Muscovite lands even more before his death in 1584. His son Fedor succeeded him but died five years later without leaving a direct heir. Several men claimed the throne. Russia was plunged into chaos, a period known as the Time of Troubles.

Eventually a group of nobles decided to end the fighting and confusion. They elected a new czar, sixteen-year-old Mikhail Romanov, who ascended the throne in 1613. One of his descendants, Peter the Great, who ruled from 1682 to 1725, expanded Russian territory and power even further. He became the first Russian ruler to take the title of emperor. Catherine the Great, who ruled from 1762 to 1796, was also responsible for a large increase in Russian influence.

Exactly three hundred years after Mikhail's rise to power, his descendant Nicholas II staged a series of elaborate celebrations to honor his family's rule. Historian Orlando Figes explains one of the purposes of the celebrations: "The election of the Romanovs in 1613 was a crucial moment of national awakening, the first real act of the Russian nation state. The 'entire land' was said to have participated in the election, thus providing a popular mandate [authorization by the citizens] for the dynasty."[1]

During the 1913 celebrations, there were many performances of Russian composer Mikhail Glinka's *A Life for the Tsar*. The hero was Ivan Susanin, a peasant who deceived a group of Polish attackers trying to murder Mikhail Romanov before his coronation. The deception cost Susanin his life.

The opera, and the mythology that grew up around it, supposedly demonstrated the bond between the Russian people and the czar. The czar *was* Russia, and its people had an almost religious obligation to serve him. This obligation wasn't a burden, according to the myth. The people served him willingly.

The truth was very different. Most of the population consisted of serfs—peasants who worked the lands belonging to noblemen. In 1649 a code of laws made them nearly slaves. They lost almost all freedom of movement.

A long series of serf uprisings began, with the most serious occurring in 1773. Emilyan Ivanovich Pugachev claimed he was actually the czar. The revolt was quickly suppressed, and Pugachev was executed.

Another threat came in 1812 when French Emperor Napoleon Bonaparte invaded Russia. After occupying Moscow, he was forced to retreat. Until then, Russia had been fairly isolated from the rest of Europe. Napoleon's invasion exposed hundreds of leading Russians to Western ideas of democracy and limited monarchy. Many realized that the biggest obstacle to modernization and reform was the czar himself.

Secret revolutionary societies began emerging. Unlike serfs, they were members of the intelligentsia. Some came from the nobility.

Late in 1825 their opportunity arrived. Czar Alexander I died in November. His brother Constantine was next in line, but he didn't want to be czar. A younger brother, Nicholas, did. He proclaimed himself as Emperor Nicholas I in mid-December.

The plotters struck. They said that Constantine was legally the emperor and demanded a constitution. Nicholas summoned troops loyal to him and arrested the conspirators. Five were hanged. Hundreds more were punished. The plotters became known as Decembrists because of the month in which their rebellion was launched. Their successors continued the foment toward reform.

Nicholas's son, Alexander II, who became czar in 1855, recognized the growing pressure. Wanting to stay in control of the situation, he emancipated the serfs in 1861. It was a mixed blessing. Serfs were no longer subject to the often cruel rule of their masters. On the other hand, land ownership brought regular mortgage payments and taxes. Because they could not afford better, serfs often wound up with land that wasn't very fertile. In general, living standards hardly improved. It was obvious that the czar and the aristocracy were only interested in hanging on to their power and making themselves wealthy. By then, the ideas of Karl Marx were beginning to spread.

These conditions contributed to Alexander's assassination in 1881. His son, Alexander III, clamped down. He was a commanding presence. Once, the

In addition to the emancipation, Alexander introduced other reforms during his reign. In 1867, he sold Alaska and the Aleutian Islands to the United States.

Alexander II and the emancipation of the serfs, 1861

Austrian ambassador suggested that his country might mobilize two or three army corps against the Russians. The czar picked up a fork and twisted it into a knot. "That is what I am going to do to your two or three army corps,"[2] he replied.

On another occasion, the czar and his family were in a railroad car that flew off the tracks. The roof caved in and trapped them. The czar pushed the roof up far enough to let his family escape.[3]

His physical power translated into political power. The country was stable financially. The pace of industrialization rapidly increased. He built up the army. He seemed to be the ideal man to rule over the world's largest country, nearly twice the size of the United States. Its population of about 120 million included dozens of different ethnic groups.

Born in 1845, Alexander was still a relatively young man at his accession. Everyone anticipated a long reign for him. Some people even began comparing him to Peter the Great. Peter had built the capital city of St. Petersburg and begun the process of modernization. Perhaps Alexander would be the one to complete this process.

In 1894, Alexander died after a brief illness. He had been in power for only thirteen years.

It was a staggering blow to Russia—and especially to Nicholas, Alexander's oldest son. Nicholas did not have the physical strength of his father. More important, his father had never groomed him for his future responsibilities.

At only twenty-six years old, Nicholas was suddenly one of the most powerful men in the world. His first response to the news of his father's death did not augur good things to come. His brother-in-law Alexander recalled: "I saw tears in his blue eyes. He took me by the arm and led me downstairs to his room. We embraced and cried together. He could not collect his thoughts. He knew that he was Emperor now, and the weight of this terrifying fact crushed him.

" 'Sandro, what am I going to do?' he exclaimed, pathetically. 'What is going to happen to me . . . to all of Russia? I am not prepared to be a Czar. I never wanted to become one.' "[4]

He would have to stick it out for twenty-three years—until Vladimir Lenin and his followers violently relieved him of his duties.

Karl Marx was born in Prussia (now Germany) in 1818. At the age of seventeen he entered Bonn University. He was more interested in having a good time than in studying. His father ordered him to transfer to the University of Berlin so he would be forced to focus on his coursework. The plan worked, though not in the way his father intended. In Berlin, Marx was exposed to revolutionary ideas. One of them was that under a capitalist system, a few people become very wealthy, and nearly everyone else lives in extreme poverty.

After he left the university, because of his radical views, he couldn't get a teaching job. He turned to journalism, but his articles got him into trouble. He fled to France, where he met a fellow German, Friedrich Engels. They began collaborating on articles and books. The most famous was *Communist Manifesto*, published in 1848. A manifesto lays out the central ideas of a group. To European governments, these communist ideas threatened their existence. Marx had a difficult time finding a place to live. He spent several years moving from country to country.

Karl Marx

Finally he settled in England. He continued to write articles, but hardly any sold. He spent most of his time at the British Museum, researching capitalist societies. Engels believed completely in what Marx was doing and became his chief source of financial support. He went back to Germany and worked for his father so that he could send money regularly to Marx.

In 1867, Marx published the first volume of *Das Kapital*. In this very detailed examination of the capitalist system, he argued that eventually capitalism would fail. By this point, however, years of poverty had caught up with him. He was in ill health. His wife died late in 1881, and Karl followed in March 1883. He managed to do quite a bit of work on two other volumes of *Das Kapital* before his death. Engels completed the books and published them.

The coronation of Nicholas II and Alexandra

The ceremony took place on May 14, 1896, in the Assumption Cathedral inside Moscow's Kremlin. Artist Laurits Tuxen depicts Nicholas reciting the Symbol of Faith, or Nicene Creed. His wife Alexandra kneels to the czar's right.

CHAPTER 3

The Reluctant Monarch

The hanging of Lenin's brother in 1887 had two results. The Ulyanov family became ostracized; few people wanted to have anything to do with them. This embittered Lenin. Also, because of his infamous family name, he was expelled from the university and couldn't enroll anywhere else. He spent most of the next four years reading political books.

He moved to St. Petersburg, where he was arrested for revolutionary activities and exiled to Siberia. It was actually a comfortable existence. He had plenty of time to read and write.

Nicholas II became czar during this exile. In spite of his initial misgivings, Nicholas was fully aware of the family tradition he was inheriting. He too wanted to be an absolute ruler. However, he wasn't up to the task. He wasn't particularly smart, and he was personally weak. Even his choice of wife worked against him. He was genuinely in love with his German-born wife, Alexandra, but few people inside Russia liked her.

His reign got off to a wretched start. Tens of thousands of people jammed into a field in St. Petersburg a few days after his coronation, expecting free food and gifts. A rumor that there weren't enough gifts swept through the crowd. Everyone began jostling forward. Nearly 1,500 people were trampled to death.

Nicholas and Alexandra attended a fancy dress ball that night. Ceremonies on succeeding days went off as planned. Many people were upset at what appeared to be an unfeeling attitude from the royal family.

"Throughout his reign Nicholas gave the impression of being unable to cope with the task of ruling a vast Empire in the grips of a deepening revolutionary crisis," notes Figes. "True, only a genius could have coped with it. And Nicholas was certainly no genius. Had circumstances and his own inclinations been different, he might have saved his dynasty by moving away from autocratic rule towards a constitutional regime during the first decade of his reign, while there was still hope of . . . isolating the revolutionary movement."[1]

Instead, Nicholas insisted on trying to maintain complete power. He believed Russia was too large and too diverse for a representative form of government to work. Only a strong leader could hold the country together.

Outwardly, the country seemed at peace. Inwardly, tensions were rising. Revolutionaries continued their work. Many were in exile in other countries, where they could be more open in their activities.

In 1903, Lenin was a major figure at the Second Russian Social Democratic Labor Party Congress. The first congress had been held five years earlier in the Russian city of Minsk. Nine members attended. They were arrested.

For safety reasons, the second congress met in Brussels, Belgium. It quickly split into two factions. Both agreed that Russia had to become capitalist before a Marxist revolution could begin. One side, the Mensheviks, thought the process would take a long time. They felt it was necessary to work side by side with nonrevolutionary groups during this period.

Lenin led the other side, the Bolsheviks. He did not want to wait, nor did he want to work with anyone else to advance the cause of the revolution. He also demanded a permanent core of revolutionaries. Supporting them required money. The Bolsheviks began robbing banks. One of their chief "fund-raisers" was a young man nicknamed Koba. He later changed his name to Joseph Stalin and became a Bolshevik leader.

Another man who began his rise about this time was Grigory Rasputin, a religious figure who became closely involved with Nicholas and Alexandra. The royal couple had had four daughters. They wanted a son to serve as the next czar. Their wishes seemed to have been granted in 1904 with the birth of Alexei. Soon they realized the horrible truth: The little boy had hemophilia, a serious disorder in which blood doesn't clot normally. Even a minor fall could be fatal, because the boy could bleed to death. In desperation, they turned to Rasputin. Somehow he managed to keep the boy's disease under control. Alexandra virtually worshiped him. He became more than a miracle healer as he took on increased importance at court.

Most people were mystified by his growing clout. The royal family had never disclosed Alexei's ailment, so there seemed to be no reason for Rasputin

Born in 1904, Alexei was the fifth child and only son born to Nicholas and Alexandra. He and the rest of his family were murdered by Bolshevik gunmen when he was just fourteen.

Nicholas II and his son, Alexei

to have so much influence over the imperial family. It made people dislike Alexandra even more.

Even before Rasputin's rise, the country had to deal with a serious situation. Nicholas, like his predecessors, tried to expand Russian territory. He had his eyes on Manchuria (a part of China) and Korea. So did the Japanese. The Russo-Japanese War broke out early in 1904. As casualties began to mount, many Russians opposed the conflict. That opposition was one factor in hundreds of strikes and demonstrations held throughout the country that year.

On Sunday, January 9, 1905, an especially large demonstration assembled in front of the czar's palace in St. Petersburg. By some estimates, it included nearly 150,000 people. Nicholas's authority lay largely in the armed forces. He ordered 12,000 soldiers to confront the unarmed demonstrators. The troops opened fire. Thousands were killed or wounded in the Bloody Sunday Massacre. Three weeks later, Nicholas said he "forgave" the demonstrators for their actions. That comment did not diffuse their anger. A few days later, his uncle was assassinated by a bomb. A series of further strikes, including a mutiny on the battleship *Potemkin* in June, showed that tensions remained high.

Nicholas finally agreed to some minor reforms. He established a Duma, a sort of parliament. However, it didn't have much power. Most of the members supported Nicholas, and the Duma couldn't pass legislation.

It wasn't enough. Strikes continued. By then, workers were forming soviets, a type of council similar to modern-day labor unions. In October, one of these soviets issued a call for revolution. Its leader was twenty-six-year-old Leon Trotsky.

On the advice of his ministers, Nicholas made even more concessions. His October Manifesto promised a constitution and a democratically elected Duma. People calmed down. Two months later, when Nicholas arrested Trotsky, violence flared again.

Nicholas used his newly appointed prime minister, Peter Stolypin, to silence the revolutionaries. Thousands of Russians were executed or banished to hard labor. So many people were hanged that the nooses became known as Stolypin's neckties. In spite of the crackdown, Stolypin knew that punishing the people wouldn't reduce the country's problems. Further changes in government were necessary. One idea was to sell better land to peasants on reasonable terms. Stolypin also tried to reduce the poisonous anti-Semitism (prejudice against Jews) that had long been an official feature of Russian life. For one reason, it was hurting relations with the United States. Nicholas refused to make these changes.

Stolypin was assassinated in 1911 by a young man with connections to the secret police. Taking advantage of his death, Nicholas reduced the powers of the prime minister. The government continued to drift.

In 1912, Lenin, who had long been in exile in Switzerland, called another party congress. At this meeting, the Bolsheviks and Mensheviks finally parted ways. Two years later, Lenin would be catapulted into world prominence.

Grigory Rasputin, a holy man, became extremely powerful in Russia in the decade before the revolution. He had some odd personal habits.

"He rose and slept and rose again without ever bothering to wash himself or change his clothes," reports historian Robert Massie. "His hands were grimy, his nails black, his beard tangled and encrusted with debris. His hair was long and greasy. Parted loosely in the middle, it hung in thin strands to his shoulders. Not surprisingly, he gave off a powerful, acrid odor."[2]

Grigory was born in Siberia in 1872. As a young man, he indulged in drinking, fighting, and love affairs. Then he claimed to have had a religious vision. He left home for two years, walking 2,000 miles to sacred Mount Athos in Greece. When he returned, he had an aura about him. This aura was aided by his deep and piercing eyes. He began developing a reputation as a healer and a preacher.

This reputation preceded him when he arrived in St. Petersburg in 1903. The church quickly welcomed him. It was trying to strengthen its ties with peasants, and Rasputin appeared to be a holy peasant.

High society also welcomed him. He was different from the well-dressed members of the nobility. Some women found him oddly appealing because of his vile personal hygiene. Others believed that his filthiness showed that he was genuinely divine.

His unique bond with Alexei cemented his status with the royal family. Eyewitness testimonies tell how he brought the boy back from what appeared to be certain death from uncontrolled bleeding. To Alexandra, he was the answer to her prayers.

From there, it was only a short step to consulting him on other affairs. He seemed almost like a member of the family. His once-shabby wardrobe improved—though he still rarely changed his clothes. As he continued to rise in importance, he attracted many enemies who were jealous of his influence. Eventually they would take action against the "mad monk."

Grigory Rasputin (center, wearing white shirt) surrounded by a gathering of his followers

Gavrilo Princip (center) is arrested after assassinating Archduke Franz Ferdinand and his wife, Sophie.

An earlier assassination attempt on the same day had failed. Princip was in a store when the driver of the car with Franz Ferdinand and Sophie took a wrong turn and drove past the store. Princip ran out and shot at them.

The Bolsheviks Take Over

On June 28, 1914, Archduke Franz Ferdinand—the heir to the throne of the empire of Austria-Hungary—and his wife, Sophie, were touring the Bosnian town of Sarajevo. A man named Gavrilo Princip bolted from the crowd and shot the royal couple.

Princip was from neighboring Serbia, which had been trying to achieve its independence from Austria-Hungary. The empire's leaders thought the assassination offered an excellent pretext to get tough with Serbia. They issued a series of harsh demands to Serbia near the end of July.

Russia supported Serbia. Germany backed Austria-Hungary. England and France joined Russia. By early August, World War I was under way.

Marxists had mixed feelings about war. They hated the thought that workers of different nations would be shooting each other, yet they thought that the chaos of war could bring down existing governments.

Russia suffered a major defeat in August 1914 at the Battle of Tannenberg. Because of anti-German sentiment, St. Petersburg, which sounded too "German," was renamed Petrograd.

In 1915, the czar decided to command the troops personally, even though he had little military experience and it would take him away from the capital. In his absence, the empress Alexandra became more influential in running the government. That, in turn, gave Rasputin even more power.

Because the army's need for supplies and transportation took priority over the needs of civilians, living conditions inside Russia steadily worsened. Battlefield casualties soared into the hundreds of thousands. There were increasing calls to abandon the war.

The Germans were aware of the dissatisfaction in Russia. It was in their interest to encourage it. They were fighting on two fronts, including Russia in the east. Getting Russia out of the war would allow hundreds of thousands of German troops to move to the Western Front and fight for victory there.

Russian leaders were just as concerned about the war. They knew it made Nicholas even more unpopular. Some of them came up with a plan late in 1916 to get rid of Rasputin and end his influence on the royal family. One plotter was Felix Yusupov, a young nobleman who married the daughter of the czar's favorite sister. He explained that the empress's "spiritual balance depends entirely on Rasputin: the instant he is gone, it will disintegrate. And once the Emperor has been freed of his wife's and Rasputin's influence, everything will change: he will turn into a good constitutional monarch."[1] As a "good constitutional monarch," Nicholas would almost certainly become more popular, which would increase the likelihood of winning the war. It would also enable Nicholas to remain on his throne, though without much of the power to which he had been accustomed.

Yusupov lured Rasputin to his home in mid-December. He and several other men poisoned him, shot him, and beat him. They wrapped his body in a carpet with ropes and chains and threw it into the Neva River.

Yusupov had made a colossal misjudgment. "I am ashamed before Russia that the hands of my relatives should be smeared with the blood of this peasant,"[2] Nicholas said. He became more resistant to the idea of changing.

The winter of 1916–1917 was severe, even by Russian standards. People suffered a great deal. Food and fuel for factories were in short supply. Though Nicholas was blamed, the country was relatively quiet.

"There were not, in the winter of 1917, any serious revolutionary plans among either workers or revolutionaries," writes historian Robert Massie. "Lenin, living in Zurich [Switzerland] in the house of a shoemaker, felt marooned, depressed and defeated. Nothing he tried seemed to succeed. . . . [Alexander] Kerensky, the Duma's most vociferous advocate of revolution, said later, 'No party of the Left and no revolutionary organization had made any plan for a revolution.' "[3]

Kerensky was the son of Fedor Kerensky, Lenin's one-time headmaster. Like Lenin, he wanted a revolution, but he wasn't as extreme. As a prominent member of the Duma, he had an official status and public recognition. Lenin, on the other hand, was relatively unknown inside Russia because he had lived out of the country for so long.

Nicholas had rushed home to console his wife after Rasputin's murder. He returned to the front lines on February 22. The following day the temperature in Petrograd climbed. The sun shone, bringing out masses of people who had been cooped up all winter. Many women lined up to receive bread. Some who grew tired of waiting broke into bakeries and took what they needed. Others paraded through the streets, shouting, "Give us bread!" Thousands of workers joined them.

For the next couple of days, more people poured into the streets. From the palace at Tsarskoe Selo, just south of Petrograd, the empress dismissed what was going on. "This is simply a hooligan movement, young people run & shout that there is no bread, simply to create excitement, along with the workers who prevent others form working," she wrote to Nicholas. "If the weather were very cold they would probably all stay home."[4]

Nicholas sent an order to General S. S. Khabalov, the city's military commander, to end the demonstrations. From his headquarters at Mogilev, hundreds of miles from Petrograd, Nicholas didn't realize how serious the situation was. According to what his wife and cabinet ministers were telling him, this was just another of the hundreds of strikes that had occurred during his reign.

On February 26, soldiers tried to clear the streets. The demonstrators ignored them. Khabalov ordered more soldiers out of their barracks. Most were either teenagers or older men with minimal training and discipline. In the late afternoon, some of them fired into a crowd. About fifty people were killed. More people were gunned down elsewhere in the city. The citizens of Petrograd were outraged, as were many soldiers.

The next morning, a regiment of soldiers chased their officers away and marched into the street to join the demonstrators. Other regiments followed. By nightfall, an estimated 60,000 soldiers had gone to the other side.

Nicholas's younger brother, Grand Duke Mikhail, wrote to the emperor, urging him to appoint a new government to deal with the situation. Nicholas replied that he would go to Tsarskoe Selo and make a decision there.

Czar Nicholas II was no longer in a position to make any decisions. His cabinet ministers had abandoned their seats. A mob of soldiers and workers swarmed into the Duma building. Its leaders agreed to accept the responsibility of the government. Soon there was another player: the Soviet of Soldiers' and Workers' Deputies. It consisted of representatives from the regiments that had mutinied and the workers who had mobbed the streets. The creation of this so-viet was largely Kerensky's idea. It represented the bulk of the city's population. He wanted to include them in the new government.

Nicholas was trying to get back to Petrograd. He couldn't. Even his personal guards deserted him. The Duma was demanding his abdication. Nicholas asked his generals for advice. They agreed with the Duma.

Nicholas realized that if he didn't abdicate, the country could be plunged into civil war. If that happened, Germany would take advantage of the chaos and easily defeat them. Like most Russians, Nicholas was patriotic. He didn't want that to happen.

He abdicated on March 15, and he included his son Alexei, who normally would have succeeded him. The boy's health could not stand up to the strain of rule, especially under these circumstances. Next in line was Nicholas's brother Mikhail. He wanted no part of the turbulence either and abdicated the following day. It was the end of the Romanov Dynasty.

A Provisional Government was quickly formed, under the direction of Prime Minister Prince Georgii Lvov. It consisted of members of both the Duma and the soviets.

The Germans were delighted with the czar's fall, but the new government seemed intent on continuing the war in spite of the war's unpopularity. In early April, the United States declared war on Germany.

With both sides reeling after nearly three years of struggle, the entry of the United States, with its vast population and industrial capacity, would almost certainly tip the balance in the Allies' favor. However, the U.S. Army was among the smallest in the world. It would take a year to raise more than two million soldiers, equip and train them, and send them overseas. That lull gave the Germans time to take advantage of the unsettled conditions in Russia. They knew the new Provisional Government wasn't firmly established. They wanted to help bring it down.

They approached Lenin, who wanted to become involved in the revolution but was stuck in Switzerland. Hundreds of miles of German territory lay between him and Russia. The Germans knew Lenin was opposed to the new government and wanted to overthrow it, so they made a deal. They would get him back home and provide him with millions of dollars in gold. He boarded a special sealed train and arrived in Petrograd on April 16.

He spoke to his Bolshevik followers and urged a new revolution. This one would establish a "dictatorship of the proletariat," or the working class. Lenin had no intention of allowing the proletariat to choose their leaders. Instead, the leaders would dictate to the proletariat.

In July, a rumor that Lenin and other Bolsheviks were pro-German began circulating. Coupled with recent Russian success on the battlefield, it forced most of the Bolsheviks to hide. Trotsky was arrested. Lenin fled to Finland. Once again he was removed from the main events.

Western Russia in 1917

It was a short-lived respite for the Provisional Government.

Lvov resigned as prime minister on July 20. Kerensky replaced him. He wanted to get rid of the Bolsheviks entirely. He ordered General Lavr Kornilov to come to Petrograd and restore order. That was a mistake. Kornilov supported the conservatives and monarchists. He wanted to take over the government and get rid of Kerensky as well. Kerensky appealed to the workers and the soviets to save the government. He released Trotsky, who helped organize the defense of the city.

In the short run, Kerensky was successful. Most of Kornilov's men refused to fight against their fellow Russians. Kornilov surrendered.

The result was a huge increase in popular support for the Bolsheviks. Many people didn't like any of the alternatives they had been given so far. Kerensky's popularity began to fade. Tens of thousands of people joined the Bolshevik party by mid-September. The party gained control of the two largest soviets, in Petrograd and Moscow, and pledged to end the war.

Lenin secretly returned to Petrograd in early October and pushed for a takeover of the government. Remembering their failure in July, many leading Bolsheviks opposed the move. Despite the gains in party membership, they weren't sure they were powerful enough.

Lenin fumed at the delay. He called a meeting of the party's Central Committee on October 10. Soviets from all over Russia were scheduled to meet for a Congress of Soviets in Petrograd on October 25, and Lenin urged a takeover just before that meeting. He was afraid to wait until the Congress had begun, since Bolsheviks were a minority in the Congress. If the Congress controlled the takeover of the government, it could proceed in a different direction than what the Bolsheviks wanted. On the other hand, if the Bolsheviks presented the Congress with an actual takeover, the Congress would likely support what they had done.

The Bolsheviks still had to justify the overthrow. As Trotsky explained, "Our strategy was offensive. We prepared to assault the government, but our agitation rested on the claim that the enemy was getting ready to disperse the Congress of Soviets and it was necessary mercilessly to repulse him."[5]

This claim of an enemy at the ready had a partial basis in fact. A German naval operation in the eastern Baltic Sea in early October threatened Petrograd. The government was considering fleeing to Moscow and reestablishing itself there. The Petrograd Soviet opposed the move and formed the Military-Revolutionary Committee (MRC).

The main objective of the MRC was to take control of the Petrograd garrison, or at least insure that most of the troops remained neutral in the upcoming showdown with the Provisional Government. The Bolsheviks knew that they had enough soldiers in the garrison who firmly supported them to overthrow the Provisional Government—as long as the remainder didn't take sides.

The Provisional Government played into their hands. Despite Kerensky's urgings, it decided not to arrest the members of the MRC. Nor did it appeal to the loyalty of the army. In fact, Kerensky even announced plans to send most of the Petrograd garrison to the front lines to meet the German threat.

The MRC immediately claimed that Kerensky's move was an attack on the upcoming Congress of Soviets. Abandoning the capital would close down the Congress and destroy the revolution, they said.

Lenin fled from Petrograd in July 1917. He changed his name to Vilén, and hid for more than a month in a hut north of the city before escaping into Finland. He returned to Russia in early October and took control of the Bolshevik Party.

Lenin fled to Finland in disguise. He shaved his beard, and wore a wig and cap.

In other words, the MRC said that they were acting in defense of the soviets. Most of the soldiers believed them. They refused to accept the authority of the Provisional Government. MRC members fanned out into the garrison and took over the leadership of most of the individual units.

"On 21 October the MRC proclaimed itself the ruling authority of the garrison: it was the first act of the insurrection,"[6] notes Figes.

The Provisional Government tried to compromise with the MRC. It was too late. In a final desperate measure on the morning of October 24, it dispatched a relative handful of troops—many of them inexperienced—to guard important points. At the same time it also shut down two Bolshevik newspapers.

Acting almost spontaneously later in the day, thousands of Bolshevik soldiers and workers began taking over key positions in Petrograd, easily brushing aside the Provisional Government guards.

They surrounded the palace where the Provisional Government was meeting. There was virtually no resistance. Kerensky, its leader, fled. The following evening, the Bolsheviks captured the palace and a few remaining government ministers. What had been an almost bloodless revolution was nearly over in about 24 hours.

The revolution wasn't quite complete. Some Congress members criticized what the Bolsheviks had done. They were also angry that the Bolsheviks had carried out their plans in the name of the Petrograd Soviet, which didn't want to have anything to do with it.

"At the Congress, the Bolsheviks called for the transfer of power to the workers', soldiers' and peasants' soviets throughout the country," observes historian Sheila Fitzpatrick. "As far as central power was concerned, the logical implication was surely that the place of the old Provisional Government would be taken by the standing Central Executive Committee of the Soviets, elected by the Congress and including representatives from a number of political parties."[7]

The implication was wrong. On October 26, the Congress announced the formation of the Council of People's Commissars. Lenin was the leader of the council. The council was supposed to be temporary, until a Constituent Assembly could be held. That never happened. The council remained in place.

The Bolsheviks had seized control of the Russian government. Their troubles were just beginning.

Lev Davidovich Bronstein—who would become Leon Trotsky—was born in 1879 to a wealthy Jewish farming family in the Ukraine. He quickly established a reputation as a good student, and he didn't become involved in revolutionary politics until 1896. His activities soon attracted attention, and he was deported to Siberia in 1900. He escaped two years later, using the name Trotsky (the name of one of his guards) on his forged passport.

He settled in London, where he became acquainted with Lenin and other members of the Russian Social Democratic Labor Party (RSDLP). The following year, at the Second RSDLP Congress, the two men split—Lenin with the Bolsheviks and Trotsky with the Mensheviks. Trotsky returned to Russia in 1905 and helped form the first soviet, a council of workers. Because the soviet opposed the czar, Trotsky was arrested and exiled for life to Siberia in 1907. After escaping again, he spent most of the next decade abroad, trying to bring the factions of the RSDLP back together.

When the Russian Revolution broke out in 1917, he was in New York. He hurried back to Russia to participate. He and Lenin quickly settled their differences. By the end of that year it was evident that he was second to Lenin in the Bolshevik party.

Trotsky became very important during the counterrevolution. He is credited with founding the Red Army. After a power struggle between Stalin and Trotsky, Stalin emerged victorious. Trotsky was forced to leave what had become known as the Soviet Union. Though he continued to write letters and articles opposing Stalin, he had a hard time find-

Leon Trotksy reading a newspaper. A picture of Lenin is on the front page.

ing a country that would allow him to live there. A famous painter, Diego Rivera, finally helped Trotsky find a permanent residence in Mexico.

Trotsky still could not escape Stalin's long reach. On August 20, 1940, an assassin broke into his office and struck him in the head with an ice ax. Trotsky died the following day.

The Bolsheviks speak at a meeting of soldiers in Petrograd in 1917.

After the takeover, the Bolsheviks still had a lot of work to do to keep the country together.

Defending the Revolution

With the Bolsheviks in control of the government, Lenin was in charge of the country. He had nearly as much power as the deposed czar had enjoyed.

Within three weeks the new government negotiated a truce with the Germans. This was in direct violation of Russia's pledge to its allies not to make a separate peace. The German terms were harsh. When the Russians signed the Treaty of Brest-Litovsk on March 3, 1918, they had to give up territory in the western part of the country, some of which they had held for more than 200 years. It included Poland, Finland, the Ukraine, Lithuania, Latvia, Estonia, and Transcaucasia.[1] It was the largest surrender of territory in Russian history. With the stroke of a pen the country lost 26 percent of its population and 37 percent of its wheat harvest.[2]

By then the Russians were experiencing trouble from within. Counter-revolutions from a number of different factions broke out. Most of these factions collectively became known as White Russians. Russia was embroiled in civil war.

One of the civil war's victims was the royal family. On July 17, 1918, the Romanovs were taken to the cellar of the house where they had been held for two and a half months. A dozen heavily armed men opened fire. All seven members of the family, the family doctor, and three servants were shot to death. Even the pet dog was killed. Most historians believe that Lenin issued the fatal order.

To Western nations, the Bolshevik victory was a disaster. They were afraid that what was now known as communism (the Bolsheviks officially changed their name to the Communist Party in March 1918) might spread to their own countries. They wanted to help the White Russians. Thousands of troops from Britain, France, Japan, and the United States landed in Russia. Many remained there for a year or even longer.

On the other hand, the Russian withdrawal from the world war had cost the Allies dearly. The Germans transferred many troops to the west and launched an offensive in March 1918. Only when American soldiers arrived later that year did the Allies win the war. Under the terms of the surrender agreement, Germany had to give up all the territory it had conquered during the war. That included the Russian lands that they had acquired through the Treaty of Brest-Litovsk.

Recovery of all that territory raised the stakes in the civil war. The White Russians were crippled with too many objectives. The Bolsheviks were united by a single purpose: to remain in power. After thousands of deaths on both sides, the fighting finally ended late in 1920. The Bolsheviks remained in control. However, another conflict began. Stalin and Trotsky—both of whom were very important in the new government—bitterly hated each other.

Joseph Stalin (left) sits next to Vladimir Lenin.

The closeness that the two men showed in March 1919 would last only a few more years. Lenin grew alarmed at Stalin's rapid rise but could do little to stop it.

Lands Affected by Treaty of Brest-Litovsk

The Treaty of Brest-Litovsk of 1918 forced Russia to give up important territory to Germany. The lands the Russians lost included a great deal of the country's industries and natural resources. After the war, Germany had to return this land.

Victory parade by German and Finnish White Guard troops in Helsinki

Influenced by events in Russia, Finland erupted in civil war in 1917. With German aid, the White Guard defeated the worker-oriented Red Guard by May 1918.

Lenin had been seriously wounded by a would-be assassin in 1918. In a wave of counter-terror, thousands of innocent people were executed.

The injury had lasting effects on Lenin's health. He suffered a stroke in May 1922. The previous month, he had appointed Stalin as general secretary of the Communist Party. At the time, it didn't seem like an important position. Stalin was even contemptuously referred to as "Lenin's mouthpiece." After the stroke, being "Lenin's mouthpiece" was an advantage. Stalin forced many of Trotsky's supporters out of the party and promoted many of his own followers. He formed the Soviet Union, which consisted of Russia and three neighboring republics: Transcaucasia, the Ukraine, and Byelorussia. (By 1956, the Soviet Union would grow to include 15 republics).

Lenin didn't approve of what Stalin was doing. After suffering a second stroke, he wrote several notes that became known as Lenin's Testament. On December 24, 1923, he noted that Stalin had "concentrated enormous power in his hands: and I am not sure that he always knows how to use that power with sufficient caution."[3] On January 4, he was even more direct. "Stalin is too rude and this defect, although quite tolerable in our midst and in dealings between Communists, becomes intolerable in a General Secretary," he wrote. "For this reason I suggest that the comrades think about a way to remove Stalin from that post and replace him with someone who has only one advantage over Comrade Stalin, namely greater tolerance, greater loyalty, greater courtesy and consideration to comrades, less capriciousness, etc."[4]

Stalin suppressed the testament. By the time it was made public a few years later, he had become so powerful that Lenin's wishes were disregarded.

Lenin died on January 21, 1924. Three days later the name of Petrograd was changed to Leningrad in his honor. Joseph Stalin's control over his country was complete.

The following year, Stalin ordered that the city of Volgograd be renamed Stalingrad in his honor. He began a ruthless dictatorship. No one knows how many people were executed on his orders, but estimates run into the millions. One of the men responsible for the killings said in 1936, "We must execute not only the guilty. Execution of the innocent will impress the masses even more."[5]

Writer Nadezhda Mandelstam had firsthand experience of Stalin's "justice system" after her poet husband was arrested; he died in prison. She adds: "The principles and aims of mass terror have nothing in common with ordinary police work or with security. The only purpose of terror is intimidation. To plunge the whole country into a state of chronic fear, the number of victims must be raised to astronomical levels, and on every floor of every building there must always be several apartments from which the tenants have suddenly been taken away. The remaining inhabitants will be model citizens for the rest of their lives."[6]

Many of the dead included army officers. Stalin had become convinced that they were planning to depose him. Their replacements knew more about communist ideas than military tactics. During World War II, when German dictator Adolf Hitler invaded Russia in 1941, he nearly defeated the Red Army. The German advance was finally checked at Stalingrad in a six-month battle that began in the late fall of 1942. More than two million soldiers and civilians died.

After the war ended in 1945, Stalin added several Eastern European nations to the Soviet Empire. His leadership also spurred what became known

Very few of these men would survive the harsh conditions of a Soviet prison camp. The same was true of Soviet troops captured by the Germans.

German POWs being led to prison camps in Stalingrad in 1943

as the Cold War, which pitted Communist USSR against the Western democracies, particularly the United States and Great Britain.

At about the same time, author George Orwell wrote *Animal Farm*. In the book, Farmer Jones badly mistreats his animals. Led by the pigs and inspired by the slogan "All animals are equal,"[7] the animals rise in revolt. Farmer Jones flees. The animals find that their living and working conditions don't improve. If anything, they get worse. However, the pigs live very well and make a change to the original slogan: "All animals are equal, but some animals are more equal than others."[8] At the end, the other animals see a meeting of humans and pigs. They can't tell them apart. The book was clearly aimed at Stalin and his methods. Orwell was saying that the Russians had exchanged one form of oppression for one that was even worse.

Stalin died in 1953. For several decades afterward, changes in leadership of the Soviet Union had little effect on the Cold War. It continued until the late 1980s, when the nations in Eastern Europe demanded their independence. The Soviet Union collapsed in 1991.

The people in Chechnya have long sought independence from Russia. Russia fights to keep control of the area, fearing other territories will also try to secede.

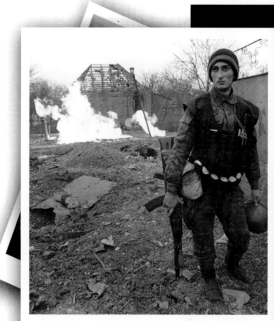

A Chechen rebel in the war with Russia

To many people, the Russian Revolution is associated with the Bolshevik takeover at the end of 1917. But the real Russian Revolution was the one that began in February of that year. It was a genuine popular revolution. Had it succeeded, Russia probably would have established a moderately democratic government. The rest of the twentieth century would have developed in a much different manner.

Instead of a popular revolt, a small group of Bolsheviks overthrew the closest thing that Russia would have to a democracy for more than seventy years. Uncounted millions of people, both inside and outside Russia, paid the price.

In a sense, the Russian Revolution is still not over. The czars are long gone. The country is no longer ruled by the communists. But democracy has had a difficult time gaining traction. Internal conflicts, especially in places such as Chechnya, have slowed the process. Economic development has been slow. No one knows what the future will bring for the largest nation on earth.

Soviet dictator Joseph Stalin was born as Joseph Vissarionovich Dzhugashvili in the Russian region of Georgia in December 1879. His family was poor, and the boy endured grinding poverty. His father drank excessively and frequently delivered harsh beatings to his wife and son. When his father deserted the family in 1888, his mother beat the little boy.

"His harsh home life left him embittered," recalled a friend of his mother. "He was an embittered, insolent, rude, stubborn child with an intolerable character."[9]

In spite of these problems, he did well in school. At fourteen, he entered a theological seminary. He became involved in revolutionary politics and, as a result, was expelled from the seminary in 1899, just before graduation. Two years later he joined the Russian Social Democratic Labor Party. He was arrested for his activities and in 1903 was sent to Siberia for a year. There, he hung out with thieves and learned their techniques.

When he returned to Georgia, he adopted the name of Koba and became a successful bank robber. He met Lenin in 1905 and gave his "earnings" to the Bolsheviks.

In 1906 he got married, though he was often on the run and spent little time with his wife. The couple had a son the following year, and his wife died soon afterward. At the funeral, he told a friend: "This being softened my heart of stone; she's passed away and with her have gone my last warm feelings for people."[10]

He put all his energy into organizing soviets, or councils, of workers. The Bolshevik leaders rewarded him by giving him the responsibility of producing their underground newspaper, *Pravda* (Truth). Soon Koba would change his name again. In 1913, he became Stalin, meaning "man of steel." The name indicated that his beliefs were strong and unshakable. It also meant that he would not allow human feelings to stand in the way of his ambitions.

Not long afterward, he was arrested and sent to Siberia. When he was finally able to return in March 1917, he quickly made up for lost time.

Timeline in History

1613	Sixteen-year-old Mikhail Romanov founds the Romanov dynasty.
1682	Peter the Great becomes czar.
1703	Peter the Great founds St. Petersburg.
1713	St. Petersburg becomes Russian capital.
1725	Peter dies.
1762	Catherine the Great becomes empress.
1796	Catherine the Great dies.
1801	Alexander I becomes emperor.
1812	Napoleon invades Russia and captures Moscow; he is forced to retreat and loses most of his army.
1825	Alexander I dies; his son Nicholas I succeeds him and crushes Decembrist uprising.
1848	Karl Marx and Friedrich Engels publish *The Communist Manifesto*.
1855	Nicholas I dies; his son Alexander II becomes emperor.
1861	Czar Alexander II frees the serfs with his Emancipation Proclamation.
1867	Marx and Engels publish first volume of *Das Kapital*.
1881	Czar Alexander II is assassinated; Alexander III becomes emperor.
1887	Vladimir (Lenin) Ulyanov's brother Alexander is hanged for plotting to kill Alexander III.
1894	Alexander III dies and his son Nicholas II succeeds him.
1903	Second Congress of Russian Social Democratic Labor Party splits into two factions: Bolsheviks and Mensheviks.
1904	Japan attacks Russian fleet based in China to begin the Russo-Japanese War; the conflict ends the following year.
1905	Bloody Sunday (January 9) marks beginning of first attempt at revolution in Russia. Sailors mutiny on the battleship *Potemkin*. Nicholas II issues October Manifesto.
1913	Elaborate celebrations mark 300th anniversary of start of Romanov dynasty.
1914	World War I begins. St. Petersburg is renamed Petrograd.
1916	Rasputin is murdered.
1917	

February 22	Workers rebel in Petrograd.
March	Nicholas II abdicates. His brother Mikhail also abdicates, ending the Romanov dynasty. Provisional Government is established.
July	Short-lived Bolshevik uprising in Petrograd ends on reports that the party's leading members are pro-German.
July 20	Alexander Kerensky becomes prime minister of the Provisional Government.
August	General Kornilov tries to take control of the Provisional Government but fails.

September	Many Russian citizens join Bolshevik party.
October 10	Lenin leads Bolshevik Central Committee in vote to overthrow Provisional Government.
October 21	Petrograd garrison falls under the control of the Bolsheviks.
October 24	Bolsheviks begin takeover of Petrograd.
October 25	Bolsheviks complete takeover of Petrograd.
October 26	Council of People's Commissars, led by Lenin, takes control of Russia.

1918

January 31	Bolshevik government adopts Gregorian calendar.
March 3	Russians sign Treaty of Brest-Litovsk.
March 8	Bolshevik Party is officially renamed Communist Party.
March 11	Government moves the Russian capital from St. Petersburg to Moscow.
July 17	Romanov family is executed.
August 30	Lenin is seriously wounded during assassination attempt.
November 11	World War I ends. Germany gives up acquired territory.

1920	White Russian uprising—Russia's civil war—ends in November.
1922	Lenin suffers stroke; Stalin becomes more powerful and forms Soviet Union.
1924	Lenin dies; Petrograd is renamed Leningrad. Stalin's power becomes total.
1925	Volgograd is renamed Stalingrad.
1937	Stalin's purges reach their peak.
1939	German dictator Adolf Hitler and Soviet dictator Joseph Stalin sign nonaggression pact; World War II begins with the German invasion of Poland.
1941	Germany invades the Soviet Union.
1943	Germans surrender at Stalingrad.
1945	World War II ends.
1953	Stalin dies.
1956	New Soviet leader Nikita Khrushchev begins program of de-Stalinization.
1963	Cuban Missile Crisis nearly causes open war between the United States and the Soviet Union.
1985	Mikhail Gorbachev becomes last general secretary of the Soviet Union.
1991	Soviet Union collapses; Russia is once again an independent republic.
2007	Russian President Vladimir Putin, who has already served two terms as president and legally cannot run for a third term, announces his plan to run in parliamentary elections in December.

Chapter Notes

**Chapter 1   The Death of
a Brother**

1. Orlando Figes, *A People's
Tragedy: The Russian Revolution, 1891–
1924* (New York: Penguin Books, 1996),
p. 139.

2. Dmitri Volkogonov, *Lenin: A New
Biography*, translated by Harold
Shukman (New York: The Free Press,
1994), p. 16.

3. Figes, p. 142.

4. Ibid, p. 166.

**Chapter 2   The Roots of
Revolution**

1. Orlando Figes, *A People's
Tragedy: The Russian Revolution, 1891–
1924* (New York: Penguin Books, 1996),
p. 11.

2. Robert Massie, *Nicholas and
Alexandra* (New York: Atheneum, 1967),
pp. 9–10.

3. David Warnes, *Chronicle of the
Russian Tsars* (New York: Thames and
Hudson, 1999), pp. 194–195.

4. Massie, p. 43.

**Chapter 3   The Reluctant
Monarch**

1. Orlando Figes, *A People's
Tragedy: The Russian Revolution, 1891–
1924* (New York: Penguin Books, 1996),
p. 19.

2. Robert Massie, *Nicholas and
Alexandra* (New York: Atheneum, 1967),
p. 190.

**Chapter 4   The Bolsheviks
Take Over**

1. Richard Pipes, *A Concise History
of the Russian Revolution* (New York:
Alfred A. Knopf, 1995), p. 73.

2. Ibid., p. 74

3. Robert Massie, *Nicholas and
Alexandra* (New York: Atheneum, 1967),
pp. 398–399.

4. Pipes, p. 77.

5. Ibid., p. 141.

6. Orlando Figes, *A People's
Tragedy: The Russian Revolution, 1891–
1924* (New York: Penguin Books, 1996),
p. 481.

7. Sheila Fitzpatrick, *The Russian
Revolution* (New York: Oxford University
Press, 1994), p. 65.

**Chapter 5   Defending the
Revolution**

1. Richard Pipes, *A Concise History
of the Russian Revolution* (New York:
Alfred A. Knopf, 1995), p. 175.

2. Ibid.

3. Orlando Figes, *A People's
Tragedy: The Russian Revolution, 1891–
1924* (New York: Penguin Books, 1996),
p. 800.

4. Ibid.

5. Pipes, p. 224.

6. Nadezhda Mandelstam, *Hope
Against Hope: A Memoir* (New York:
Modern Library, 1999), p. 358.

7. George Orwell, *Animal Farm*
(New York: Signet Books, 1996), p. 43.

8. Ibid., p. 133.

9. Edvard Radzinsky, *Stalin*,
translated by H.T. Willetts (New York:
Doubleday, 1996), p. 23.

10. Robert Service, *Stalin: A
Biography* (Cambridge, Massachusetts:
Harvard University Press, 2005), p. 70.

Glossary

abdicate (AB-dih-kayt)
To step down.

aliases (AY-lee-us-es)
Different names that a person takes to disguise his or her identity.

augur (AW-gur)
Predict the future on the basis of one or more current events.

barracks (BAYR-eks)
Buildings in which soldiers live.

constitutional monarch (kon-stih-TOO-shuh-nul MAH-nark)
A ruler who shares his or her power with a legislative body under the legal terms of a constitution.

emancipated (ee-MAN-sih-pay-ted)
Set free from slavery or servitude.

industrialization (in-dus-tree-uh-ly-ZAY-shun)
The changing of a society from farming to factory work (industry).

intelligentsia (in-tel-ih-JEN-shya)
The educated class in a society.

mandate (MAN-dayt)
An authorization to perform certain acts.

ostracized (OS-truh-syzd)
Excluded from a group; shunned.

popular (PAH-pyoo-lur)
Coming from people in the general population.

purge (PURJ)
The often violent removal of people thought to be disloyal.

soviet (SOH-vee-et)
A council of workers.

vociferous (voh-SIH-fuh-rus)
Especially loud and demanding; outspoken.

Further Reading

For Young Adults

Cunningham, Kevin. *Joseph Stalin and the Soviet Union.* Greensborough, North Carolina: Morgan Reynolds, 2006.

Gottfried, Ted. *The Road to Communism.* Brookfield, Connecticut: Twenty-First Century Books. 2002.

Murrell, Kathleen Berton. *Eyewitness Books: Russia.* New York: Dorling Kindersley, 1998.

Naden, Corinne J., and Rose Blue. *The Importance of Lenin.* San Diego, California: Lucent Books, 2003.

Orwell, George. *Animal Farm.* New York: Signet Books, 1996.

Works Consulted

Figes, Orlando. *A People's Tragedy: The Russian Revolution, 1891–1924.* New York: Penguin Books, 1996.

Fitzpatrick, Sheila. *The Russian Revolution.* New York: Oxford University Press, 1994.

Mandelstam, Nadezhda. *Hope Against Hope: A Memoir.* New York: Modern Library, 1999.

Massie, Robert. *Nicholas and Alexandra.* New York: Atheneum, 1967.

Orwell, George. *Animal Farm.* New York: Signet Books, 1996.

Pipes, Richard. *A Concise History of the Russian Revolution.* New York: Alfred A. Knopf, 1995.

Radzinsky, Edvard. *Stalin.* Translated by H.T. Willetts. New York: Doubleday, 1996.

Service, Robert. *Stalin: A Biography.* Cambridge, Massachusetts: Harvard University Press, 2005.

Volkogonov, Dmitri. *Lenin: A New Biography.* Translated by Harold Shukman. New York: The Free Press, 1994.

Warnes, David. *Chronicle of the Russian Czars.* New York: Thames and Hudson, 1999.

On the Internet

"Alexander Kerensky" http://www.spartacus.schoolnet.co.uk/RUSkerensky.htm

Beéche, Arturo. "The Evil Monk: The Life and Times of Gregory Efimovich Rasputin." http://www.eurohistory.com/site/Rasputin.html

The Great War—Historians—Orlando Figes http://www.pbs.org/greatwar/historian/hist_figes_01_rasputin.html

"Karl Marx" http://www.spartacus.schoolnet.co.uk/TUmarx.htm

"Study Guide for the Communist Manifesto" http://www.wsu.edu:8080/~brians/hum_303/manifesto.html

Index